Date Due

NOV 1 5 2000			
NOV 2 6 2002			

BRODART, CO.   Cat. No. 23-233-003   Printed in U.S.A.

❧ PROFILES OF GREAT ❧
BLACK AMERICANS

Book of Firsts: Sports Heroes

❧❧

Edited by Richard Rennert

Introduction by Coretta Scott King

⫼⫼ A Chelsea House
⫼⫼ Multibiography

Chelsea House Publishers
New York Philadelphia

On the cover: Arthur Ashe serves at Forest Hills.

3   5   7   9   8   6   4   2

Library of Congress Cataloging-in-Publication Data

Book of Firsts: Sports Heroes/edited by Richard Rennert
p. cm.—(Profiles of great Black Americans)
(A Chelsea House multibiography)
Includes bibliographical references and index.
ISBN   0-7910-2055-X.
            0-7910-2056-8 (pbk.)
    1. Afro-American athletes—Biography—Juvenile literature.
I. Rennert, Richard. II. Series. III. Series: A Chelsea House
multibiography
GV697.A1B576 1993   93-18437
796'.092'2—dc20   CIP
[B]   AC

❧ CONTENTS ❧

❧ INTRODUCTION ❧

by Coretta Scott King

This book is about black Americans who served society through the excellence of their achievements. It forms a part of the rich history of black men and women in America—a history of stunning accomplishments in every field of human endeavor, from literature and art to science, industry, education, diplomacy, athletics, jurisprudence, even polar exploration.

Not all of the people in this history had the same ideals, but I think you will find something that all of them had in common. Like Martin Luther King, Jr., they all decided to become "drum majors" and serve humanity. In that principle—whether it was expressed in books, inventions, or song—they found something outside themselves to use as a goal and a guide. Something that showed them a way to serve others instead of only living for themselves.

Reading the stories of these courageous men and women not only helps us discover the principles that we will use to guide our own lives but also teaches us about our black heritage and about America itself. It is crucial for us to know the heroes and heroines of our history and to realize that the price we paid in our struggle for equality in America was dear. But we must also understand that we have gotten as far as we have partly because America's democratic system and ideals made it possible.

We are still struggling with racism and prejudice. But the great men and women in this series are a tribute to the spirit of our democratic ideals and the system in which they have flourished. And that makes their stories special and worth knowing.

Champion of the tennis courts and of social issues, Arthur Robert Ashe, Jr., was born in Richmond, Virginia, on July 10, 1943. His father, Arthur, Sr., was a guard in charge of Brook Field, Richmond's largest playground. His mother, Mattie, died of complications during her third pregnancy when Arthur was six years old, leaving her husband to raise Arthur and his younger brother, John.

A strict disciplinarian, Mr. Ashe taught his sons the importance of self-reliance and self-discipline, two traits that would later prove essential to Arthur. Arthur first picked up a tennis racket at the age of six on the courts at Brook Field. Though childhood illnesses had left him with a slight build, he learned how to perfect his stroke from Ronald Charity, a top-ranked black player who worked there as an instructor.

Arthur showed such promise on the court that at the age of 10, Dr. Robert Johnson, a member of the all-black American Tennis Association (ATA) who had trained Althea Gibson, offered to train him. When Arthur was 12 years old, he won the ATA National Championship for his age group, then continued to win tournament after tournament. Nevertheless, he was disappointed when the predominantly white U.S. Lawn Tennis Association (USLTA), the sport's most important governing body, rejected his application for a junior tournament in his hometown of Richmond even though the organization then ranked him fifth among all tennis players in his age group.

In 1960, Arthur became the ATA's youngest champion ever when he won both the junior and the men's singles titles. By this time, it was clear that because Arthur was becoming one of the great black tennis players in the ATA, it was time for him to leave Richmond, where segregation laws prohibited him from playing on indoor courts, thus restricting his court time to the summer and hindering his development.

That year, Ashe was sent to Sumner High School in St. Louis, Missouri, where he could play tennis indoors in the winter and compete in tournaments during the spring and summer. In November, he became the first black to win the National Juniors Indoor Tournament when he upset the top-seeded player in a four-and-a-half-hour marathon match. His equally committed dedication to his studies paid off also; that spring he graduated from Sumner first in his class. His grades and tennis skills allowed him to become the first black to receive a tennis scholarship to the University of California at Los Angeles (UCLA).

At UCLA, Ashe majored in business administration. While a student there, he represented the United States several times as a member of the Davis Cup team, participated for the first time in the All-England Championships at Wimbledon, and improved his standing in the world amateur rankings from 28th to 6th. In 1964 he was given the Johnston Award, which is voted annually to that individual who contributes the most to the game while exhibiting good sportsmanship and character. For Ashe, the award carried an additional significance: after years of discrimination, blacks were finally being accepted in the tennis world.

By 1965, Ashe was the top-ranked collegiate tennis player in America. He continued to be a driving force for the Davis Cup team, and he played well at both

Wimbledon and the U.S. National Championships at Forest Hills, New York, although he failed to win either title. His hometown proclaimed February 4, 1966, Arthur Ashe Day, and the city where he had once been prohibited from playing on all-white tennis courts honored him with a banquet and a ceremony at city hall.

After graduating from UCLA in June 1966, Ashe fulfilled his two-year ROTC commitment to the U.S. Army as assistant tennis coach at the U.S. Military Academy at West Point. Though his military obligation played havoc with his tournament schedule, he still rose to the number-two ranking among U.S. amateurs.

Nineteen sixty-eight proved to be a banner year for Ashe. After a strong showing at Wimbledon, Ashe became the first black man to win a Grand Slam tournament when he won the first U.S. Open at Forest Hills, thereby securing his top ranking among the world's amateurs. He followed up his victory in December by helping his teammates bring home the Davis Cup from Australia.

Upon his return to the United States, Ashe found himself in the spotlight. His picture appeared on the cover of numerous magazines, and he was courted by various companies to promote their products. It was not only his victories on the tennis courts that made him a celebrity but his involvement in social causes as well.

In 1969, Ashe and several other players created the International Tennis Players Association (ITPA) to protect the interests of tennis players. The ITPA evolved into the Association of Tennis Players (ATP) in 1972 and, with Ashe serving as vice-president, boycotted Wimbledon that year in protest over unfair treatment of a Yugoslavian member of the ATP.

Racism was another issue of importance to Ashe. In 1969, after he applied for and was refused a visa to South Africa to play tennis there, he enlisted the support of various groups; his efforts resulted in the expulsion of South Africa from the Davis Cup competition in 1970.

Because of his support of human rights issues, the U.S. government invited Ashe to speak before the African subcommittee of the House of Representatives Foreign Relations Committee. He was also invited to serve as a U.S. goodwill ambassador for a tour of Africa. When, in 1973, South Africa finally granted Ashe a visa and the opportunity to play in the South African Open, it marked the first time a black had ever competed in the event. Ashe made his appearance in the tournament even more memorable by teaming with Tom Okker to win the doubles title.

As Ashe became more involved in business and civil rights matters, his tennis game began to fall off somewhat. From 1971 to 1974, Ashe won only 11 of the 123 tournaments he entered. In 1975, at the age of 31, he came back to win the WCT championship in May, and he finally reached his goal by winning at Wimbledon, where he beat Jimmy Connors in five sets. His victories that year earned him the distinction of being ranked number one in the world—the first black male professional tennis player to attain that position.

Ashe married Jeanne Marie Moutoussamy, a professional photographer, on February 20, 1977, at the United Nations Chapel in New York City. He continued to participate in tournaments until July 1979, when his career was cut short by a heart attack. Though the tennis superstar later underwent quadruple bypass surgery to alleviate several blocked arteries, he continued to be active in the sports world as captain of the 1981 U.S. Davis Cup team and as a television commentator for the ABC and HBO networks. Ashe was also an active member of the USTA Player Development Committee, which he cofounded to promote junior tennis and to offer underpriviledged children the opportunity to play the sport.

Ashe was inducted into the Tennis Hall of Fame in Newport, Rhode Island, in 1985. In 1987, his wife, Jeanne, gave birth to their only child, a daughter, Camera Elizabeth. Ashe's other contributions included serving on the board of the American Heart Association and his authorship of several books. *A Hard Road to Glory*, his three-volume history of black American athletes, was especially well received and brought Ashe many requests to lecture at universities and colleges.

Ironically, the heart operations that saved Ashe's life ultimately robbed him of it as well. On April 8, 1992, Ashe held a press conference to announce that he had contracted acquired immune deficiency syndrome (AIDS) from a blood transfusion following heart surgery that contained the AIDS virus. Ashe revealed that he had felt compelled to make the announcement because the newspaper *USA TODAY* was about to publish the story.

Once again, Arthur Ashe found himself in the spotlight, championing another cause and fighting more discrimination. He spoke out both for his own right to privacy and that of similarly afflicted individuals, and he became active in the fight against AIDS and the ignorance and prejudice that surround the disease, forming a fund-raising foundation and joining the boards of the Harvard AIDS Institute and the UCLA AIDS Institute. Even after the announcement of his condition, Ashe continued the fight against racism and prejudice, and he was arrested and jailed in the summer of 1992 following a protest in front of the White House regarding U.S. policy on Haitian refugees.

Arthur Ashe, tennis champion, defender of human rights, and fighter against racism, contracted pneumonia, a frequent complication of AIDS, and died on February 6, 1993, in New York City. After lying in state in the governor's mansion in Richmond, Virginia, he was buried in his hometown following a funeral service in which he was praised not only for his achievements in the sport of tennis but also for his quiet dignity and unshaken beliefs.

CHUCK COOPER

Charles "Chuck" Cooper, the first African-American in the National Basketball Association (NBA), was 24 years old when he was drafted by the Boston Celtics on April 25, 1950. A solid six-foot-five-inch, 215-pound center, Cooper had been a first-team all-American at Duquesne University in Pittsburgh and had led his team to the semifinals of the prestigious National Invitational

Tournament (NIT). Nevertheless, all the owners and general managers present at the Chicago hotel where the NBA draft was held were shocked when the owner of the Celtics, Walter Brown, announced that he was making Cooper Boston's second-round pick. "Walter, don't you know he's a colored boy?" one of the other owners blurted out. To which Brown retorted, "I don't give a damn if he's striped, plaid, or polka-dot! Boston takes Chuck Cooper of Duquesne!"

Cooper's choice by the Celtics was the culmination of a long journey by black players that had begun soon after the first game of basketball was played on January 15, 1892, in Springfield, Massachusetts. By the beginning of the 20th century, black players were featured on a number of college basketball squads; the most notable of these performers was the versatile Paul Robeson of Rutgers, who went on to become a renowned singer and actor as well as a political activist. The pool of talented black players was augmented in the years following World War I, when the black colleges in the segregated South formed their own athletic conference, the Central Interscholastic Athletic Association (CIAA). Among the CIAA's members, Morgan State, Virginia Union, and Xavier of New Orleans emerged as dominant teams during the 1920s and 1930s, attracting players from the North as well as the South.

Black professional basketball teams also came into being in the early 1900s—most notably, the Incorporators and the Loendi Big Five—but the best of the black pro teams was created in 1923. In that year,

Robert L. "Bob" Douglas persuaded a fellow immigrant from the Caribbean, William Roche, to make his Harlem Renaissance Casino available for basketball games. The teams played with portable baskets, and after the game they cleared the floor so that the audience could dance to the music of a swing band. Douglas's team, the Harlem Renaissance, soon known simply as the Rens, was a dominant force from the start, ultimately compiling a record of 2,318 wins against only 381 losses. The Rens truly hit their stride during the 1930s, when they boasted such standout players as William "Pops" Gates, Fats Jenkins, Bill Yancey, and Charles "Tarzan" Cooper. Traveling from city to city on their own bus, the Rens steamrolled black and white teams alike. Opposing players and sports reporters acknowledged them as the best team in the world.

Though there were instances of black players being hired by white teams, an unofficial color line clearly existed in professional basketball. Aside from playing for the Rens, there was only one other way for black players to earn a decent living at the game—by playing for the Harlem Globetrotters. The Globetrotters, who evolved from a Chicago semipro team known as the Savoy Big Five, achieved prominence when they hired a white promoter, Abe Saperstein. With Saperstein making the contacts—and eventually running the team—the Trotters were able to get more bookings, for better money, than a team like the Rens, whose management was black.

The Globetrotters, who continued to make Chicago their home base, soon became known as much for their clowning on the court as for their considerable basketball prowess. Their ball-handling tricks and other antics made the Trotters less threatening to white spectators and took the sting out of the drub-bings they administered to all-white teams. Even though Saperstein's legacy has become a controversial one, with some regarding him as a benefactor of black players and others as an exploiter, he made a long-lasting financial success of the Globetrotters and provided a showcase for such outstanding athletes as Goose Tatum and Marcus Haynes.

During the 1940s, basketball changed from a slow-paced, grinding type of game to a more up-tempo sport that featured such innovations as the jump shot and the fast break. Black players were often at the forefront of these changes, making the most of their superior jumping ability and quickness.

When the National Basketball Association came into being in 1949, the color line still prevailed, but it had become clear that segregation in sports was on its way out. Two years earlier, Jackie Robinson had broken the color line in major league baseball when he stepped on the field for the Brooklyn Dodgers. Nevertheless, when the Celtics picked Chuck Cooper in the NBA's second player draft, the move created shock waves, and not merely among NBA owners. Abe Saperstein, fearing that his Globetrotters would no longer have first pick of the nation's best black players, threatened to cancel all his team's engagements at the Boston Garden. But Boston owner Walter Brown refused to back down, and the NBA was open to the nation's great black hoopsters.

Two rival teams quickly followed Boston's example—so quickly, in fact, that although Chuck Cooper was the first black player taken in the draft, he was neither the first to sign an NBA contract nor the first to play in an NBA game. The distinction of signing the first NBA pact belonged to Nat "Sweetwater" Clifton, whose contract was purchased from the Globetrotters (after he and Saperstein had a falling out) by the New York Knickerbockers. And the first black player to actually enter a game during the 1950 season was Earl Lloyd, who started for the Washington Caps against the Rochester Royals on October 31.

None of the three players followed the example of Jackie Robinson by achieving stardom and Hall of Fame status. Cooper's first year for the Celtics, in which he averaged 9.3 points a game and contributed a total of 562 rebounds and 174 assists, was quite respectable—but it turned out to be the best he enjoyed with the team. Too short to play center in the pros, he now had to adjust to playing forward and occasionally guard. In 1951, Cooper's scoring average fell to 8.2; it dropped still further, to 6.5, the following year. In 1954, the Celtics traded him to the Milwaukee Hawks, and in 1955–56 he moved on to play for the Fort Wayne Pistons and the St. Louis Hawks. By 1956, Cooper's NBA career was over.

In looking back on his NBA days, Cooper felt that
he was never given a fair chance to show what he could
do. He claimed that his offensive potential was over-
looked and that he was always asked to do the rebounding and tough defensive work while his white
teammates did the shooting. He also believed that his
injuries were taken less seriously than those of white
players. Interestingly, Lloyd also felt that he had been
stifled as a professional player, though he had a longer
career than Cooper, playing until 1960. Even Clifton,
whose seven-year career with the Knicks was distin-
guished by a 10.3 scoring average and a 1957 All-Star
selection, later asserted that New York management
had kept him under wraps.

After Cooper left the NBA, he spent a few seasons
with the Harlem Magicians, a team organized by
former Globetrotter Marcus Haynes. After retiring as
a player, Cooper returned to Pittsburgh, where he had
attended college, and enjoyed a successful business
career until his death in February 1984. Sweetwater
Clifton, by contrast, drove a cab in his native Chicago
for 25 years, until his death in 1990. Lloyd was the only
one of the trio who remained in the game, eventually
serving as head coach of the Detroit Pistons during the
1970s.

Before the 1950s were over, the NBA was to be all
but dominated by black stars such as Bill Russell, Wilt
Chamberlain, Elgin Baylor, and Oscar Robertson. In
1966, the NBA became the first major professional
league to feature a black head coach when Bill Russell
took the helm of the Boston Celtics. By the 1990s,

more than 70 percent of the league's players were black, and the hiring of black coaches and front-office personnel was taken for granted in the league. Though frustrated in his quest for NBA stardom, Chuck Cooper, along with fellow pioneers Earl Lloyd and Sweetwater Clifton, began the quiet revolution that has made professional basketball a model of equal opportunity in sports.

ALTHEA GIBSON

Tennis champion Althea Gibson was born on August 25, 1927, in Silver, South Carolina. Her sharecropper parents, Daniel and Annie Gibson, later moved the family to New York City in an attempt to escape the poverty and racial discrimination of the South.

A mischievous and rebellious child, Althea grew up in the predominantly black neighborhood of Harlem.

As she grew older, she was often in trouble, skipping school and getting into fights. She did, however, excel at athletics, and at the age of 13 she was discovered by a member of the community on a paddle-tennis court and taken to the Cosmopolitan Club, New York's most prestigious black tennis club, where she was given lessons.

Tennis had been introduced to the United States as a country club sport in the 1880s. Because most clubs were segregated, it had remained a predominantly white sport. In large part, the members of the Cosmopolitan Club encouraged Althea to play because they saw in her a chance to promote the participation of blacks in tennis.

A year after she started tennis lessons, Althea played in and won her first tournament, the New York State Open Championship, sponsored by the American Tennis Association (ATA), an association of black tennis players. Her victory proved to the members of the Cosmopolitan Club that Althea was a talent worth developing.

Althea continued to work on her game at the Cosmopolitan Club, and when she was 18 years old she was befriended by Sugar Ray Robinson, the celebrated boxer, who encouraged her to pursue her education and her tennis career. She was given this opportunity after two men who were interested in promoting black tennis players spotted her at an ATA competition and offered to give her the opportunity to finish high school and to continue her tennis lessons.

Terrified at first at the thought of leaving home, Althea eventually moved into the household of Dr. Hubert A. Eaton, a wealthy South Carolina doctor. While she concentrated on her studies and her tennis game, Althea was introduced to the legally sanctioned racial discrimination that was prevalent in the Deep South. She had to sit in the back of buses and was not allowed in areas marked "Whites Only." This discrimination was more overt than the discrimination she had experienced in New York.

In 1947, Gibson won all nine of the women's singles titles on the ATA circuit. Her victory at the U.S. National Championship was the beginning of her winning streak of 10 consecutive ATA National Championships. In the following years, as Althea continued to dominate black women's tennis, the ATA increased its efforts to break tennis's racial barrier. These efforts paid off in Althea's senior year of high school, with the acceptance of her entry to the Eastern Indoor Championships, an event sponsored by the U.S. Lawn Tennis Association (USLTA), which governed tennis events played by whites.

Althea played well in the tournament, advancing to the quarterfinals. The USLTA was impressed with her performance and invited her to the National Indoor Championship, in which she put in another strong showing but lost in the quarterfinal once again. During this time, Althea was also given an opportunity to achieve her other goal—the completion of her education—when Florida A & M

University offered her a full scholarship for the fall of 1949.

Although she continued to play at the USLTA indoor championships, Althea was not invited to any of its outdoor events because these were played at private, segregated country clubs. However, as she continued to play well and public interest in her increased, the USLTA's practices were brought into question. An important development in this regard came in 1950, when Alice Marble, who had dominated women's tennis in the 1930s, spoke out against racial discrimination in tennis.

Marble's article in *American Lawn Tennis* magazine shamed the USLTA into offering Althea invitations to play in their tournaments. The main event of the USLTA tour was the U.S. National Championships, held annually in Forest Hills, New York, and in August of 1950, Althea Gibson was invited to play in the tournament.

Though mobbed by curious reporters and onlookers, Gibson held her own at Forest Hills, losing in the second round to Louise Brough, the Wimbledon champion. Nonetheless, Gibson's appearance at the U.S. National Championships was a victory in itself; she had caused a media sensation and had torn down the barrier to blacks participating in USLTA events.

In 1951, Gibson broke another color barrier when she became the first black to play in the All-England Tennis Championships at Wimbledon, the most prestigious event in tennis. However, she was disappointed in her performance and was eliminated in the

third round. Over the next few years, Gibson remained a strong player on the ATA and USLTA circuits, achieving the highest ranking of her career to date in 1953, when she was ranked the seventh-best woman player in the United States.

After reaching this pinnacle, her performance began to slip, and she gradually slipped out of the public's notice. After her graduation from college, Gibson took a position as a physical education instructor at Lincoln University, a black college in racially segregated Jefferson City, Missouri. Unhappy with her career, she submitted an application to the Women's Army Corps, but these plans were put aside when the U.S. State Department asked her to participate in a goodwill tennis tour of Southeast Asia.

The tour renewed Gibson's confidence and enthusiasm for tennis. She was greatly impressed by the Far East, and she was able to concentrate on her game. At the end of the tour, Gibson chose to go to Europe to prepare for the Wimbledon championship that spring.

Gibson thus began a whirlwind tennis tour in which she swept European tennis with victories from Cannes to Monte Carlo. In May 1956, she became the first black to win a major singles title with a victory at the French Championships. However, Wimbledon once again proved to be her nemesis, and she lost in her quarterfinals match. Even though she also lost the U.S. National Championships in the finals, she had leapt from thirteenth to second in the national rankings.

In 1957, Gibson realized the dream that had eluded her for so long when she won at Wimbledon, defeating fellow American Darlene Hard in the finals. Upon her return to New York, Gibson was greeted with a ticker-tape parade and luncheons in her honor. Despite her accomplishments, Gibson was uncomfortable with her new status as a symbol of black achievement. Many blacks criticized her for letting tennis take precedence over civil rights issues and attacked her reluctance to become an outspoken representative for black people.

Her victory at the 1957 U.S. National Tennis Championships clinched her standing as the best female tennis player in the world. The following year, she shocked the tennis world when, moments after her second victory at Forest Hills, Althea Gibson announced her retirement from amateur tennis. Her reason for retiring was purely financial. Despite her many titles, Gibson's economic situation was desperate, because in those days tennis was still ostensibly an amateur sport and players were not awarded money for their titles.

In the following years, Gibson attempted to pursue singing and acting careers with modest success, but her most successful venture came in 1959, when she toured with the Harlem Globetrotters in a tennis exhibition. Her financial troubles continued when she launched a disappointing exhibition tour of her own, which left her in debt when it ended. Her salvation came in the form of another game—golf.

Gibson had first played golf in the mid-1950s, but it was not until 1962 that she considered becoming a professional. Golf was another sport pervaded by racial prejudice, but Althea became the first black woman to enter the Ladies Professional Golf Association (LPGA) in 1964. Even though the country clubs where many of the LPGA tournaments were held were racially segregated, Gibson's entrance into the LPGA was smoother than her struggle in the world of tennis. LPGA members held considerable clout and could remove from their tournament list any country club that would not admit their members. Gibson had the full support of Leonard Wirtz, director of the LPGA, who would move tournaments to other clubs in response to discrimination against Althea.

Gibson set out to prove herself on the LPGA tour, gradually improving throughout 1964 and 1965. In 1965, Gibson felt her career was stable enough to concentrate on her personal life, and she married Will Darben, a man she had known for many years. Her golf game peaked in 1967, but by the end of 1971, she realized it was time for her to retire.

Her marriage also came to an end, and in 1975, Gibson found a new home when she became the manager of the Department of Recreation in East Orange, New Jersey, a city with a large black population. She was inducted into the South Carolina Hall of Fame in 1983 and the Florida Sports Hall of Fame in 1984. She currently maintains a quiet life in East Orange, New Jersey.

JACK JOHNSON

The first black man to win the heavyweight boxing championship of the world, John Arthur "Jack" Johnson was born in Galveston, Texas, on March 31, 1878. Henry Johnson, Jack's father, was a former slave from Maryland who had also been an amateur boxer; at the time of Jack's birth, Henry Johnson made a living as a woodworker and school janitor. Jack's mother, Tina, called Tiny, was a high-spirited woman who saw that her six children went to school and church; when necessary, she kept them in line with a two-by-four.

Tall and awkward as a child, Jack was inclined to be anything but a fighter. Indeed, the neighborhood bullies found him a tempting target until his mother grew tired of seeing him pushed around. She told him that if he did not begin fighting back, he would get an even worse beating from her. Jack decided to take his chances with the bullies and found that he could thrash them easily, making use of his extraordinary hand speed.

Despite his mother's efforts, Jack quickly lost interest in school. He dropped out after the sixth grade, working at a succession of odd jobs but always dreaming of somehow making his mark in life. He began to fight for sport along Galveston's rough-and-tumble waterfront and eventually gravitated into the local boxing clubs, where he honed his skills and had his first professional bouts. In 1899, he made a brief trip to Chicago but returned home after being badly outclassed in a bout and blowing his share of the purse at the racetrack.

After living through the dreadful hurricane that destroyed much of Galveston in the summer of 1900, Johnson left home for good the following year and made his way to California. At that time, none of the leading white prizefighters would agree to a match with a black opponent, so Johnson could not even dream of reaching the upper echelons of the sport. He fought other black heavyweights, some of whom were very skilled, and by 1903 he was recognized as the best of the group. He had also developed a taste for elegant, attention-getting clothes and fast motorcars.

In 1905, Johnson finally got a fight against a leading white contender, Marvin Hart, in San Francisco. Johnson pummeled Hart over 20 rounds, but the referee awarded the decision to the white fighter. A disgusted Johnson left California for Philadelphia, where he had the first of a series of bouts with Joe Jeannette, a top-notch black fighter. In 1906, he squared off against Sam Langford, the best of the black heavyweights, and won a 15-round decision. Still frustrated by boxing's color line, Johnson then issued a public challenge to the heavyweight champion, Jim Jeffries. Jeffries's reply: "When there are no white men left to fight, I will quit the business."

In May 1905, Jeffries followed up on his vow and hung up his gloves. He arranged a series of elimination bouts among the white contenders, and Jack Burns, a smallish Canadian, emerged from the lackluster group as the new champion. Burns's lack of popularity gave Johnson an opening. Having acquired a clever manager, Sam Fitzpatrick, Johnson began a public campaign to force Burns into a fight. After disposing of a number of white fighters—including former heavyweight champion Bob Fitzsimmons, Kid Cutler, and Fireman Jim Flynn—Johnson had the press calling on Burns to settle "the matter of fistic supremacy between the white race and the colored."

Burns avoided Johnson by going on a European tour in 1907–8. Johnson sailed after him, taking on a few opponents in England, and he and Burns eventually wound up in Australia, where they signed a contract that promised Johnson a $5,000 purse. (Burns's share was $30,000.) The fight took place before 20,000 spectators on Christmas Day, 1908, in Rushcutter's Bay, a suburb of Sydney. Burns, at five feet seven inches and 175 pounds, was no match for Johnson, a muscular six-footer who weighed more than 200 pounds. Johnson decked Burns with a terrific right uppercut in the first round and could have ended the fight right there. But he chose to carry his opponent for 14 rounds, dishing out fearful punishment while both the crowd and Burns hurled racial slurs at him. When the police finally stopped the contest, Johnson had the heavyweight crown at last.

Johnson played the role of champion to the hilt, buying jewelry, automobiles, and carousing with a succession of white women. A string of "great white hopes" emerged to reclaim the title, but Johnson dispatched them all easily, taking pleasure in the cat-calls of the hostile whites who came out to see him beaten.

Johnson's detractors lived in despair until 1909, when Jim Jeffries agreed to come out of retirement and try to regain the title. The Jeffries-Johnson match took place on July 4, 1910, in Reno, Nevada, and once again Johnson proved that he was the best heavyweight boxer in the world. He completely out-classed Jeffries under the hot desert sun, showing the former champion his entire repertoire before closing in for a 15th-round knockout.

The public reaction to Johnson's victory was a sad commentary on race relations in the United States. In city after city, blacks who took to the streets in celebration were set upon by mobs of whites; when the rioting subsided, 20 people lay dead, and hundreds more were injured. The situation was so alarming that federal authorities banned the distribution and showing of the fight film.

Johnson had earned $160,000—a phenomenal sum for that time—from the Jeffries fight, and he found that he could make as much as $2,500 a week traveling the vaudeville circuit. However, the money brought him neither public acceptance nor personal contentment. In 1911, Johnson married Etta Terry Duryea, a white woman he had been living with on and off for some time. The marriage was a disaster; the following year, Duryea, tired of being an outcast among both races, shot herself to death. Johnson quickly took up with Lucille Cameron, an 18-year-old prostitute. When Cameron's mother claimed that Johnson had abducted her daughter, the U.S. Justice Department decided to take action. Even though Johnson and Cameron were married in 1912, the government induced a former lover to testify against the champion and arrested him for violating the Mann Act, a law against transporting women across state lines for prostitution.

Johnson went on trial in Chicago in May 1913. The government's case was flimsy, but an all-white jury convicted Johnson just the same: his crime, in the eyes of society, was consorting with white women. When the judge sentenced Johnson to a year and a day in prison and released him on bail pending appeal, the champion decided to flee the country.

After sailing to Europe from Canada, Johnson enjoyed his exile for a time, until he ran out of money. Then he was forced to put on boxing and wrestling exhibitions in order to get by. In 1914, as World War I broke out in Europe, Johnson agreed to defend his championship in Havana, Cuba, against Jess Willard, a six-foot-six-inch, 250-pound giant from Kansas. Johnson took a leisurely route to Cuba and did little to get his 37-year-old body into fighting trim. The bout, scheduled to go 45 rounds, took place on April 15, 1915. After 20 rounds, it became clear that Johnson could not put the challenger away, and his lack of training began to show. In the 26th, Willard delivered a right to Johnson's jaw that sent the champion to the canvas, where he was counted out.

After the Willard fight, Johnson returned to Europe for a while and then gravitated to Mexico, where he was received as a guest of President Venustiano Carranza. Carranza's overthrow soon ended his welcome, and in 1920 Johnson crossed the border into the United States and surrendered to federal authorities. He served 10 months in the penitentiary at Leavenworth, Kansas; here, at least, the authorities treated him with respect and encouraged him to put on boxing exhibitions for the other inmates.

Upon his release in 1921, Johnson traveled to New York, where he was given a hero's reception in Harlem. He spoke of getting back into the ring and reclaiming his championship, but at the age of 43 he had to content himself with being a living legend. During the 1930s and 1940s, he was frequently called into the ring for a quick bow before important fights; the crowds, which had by now learned to idolize great black champions, such as Joe Louis and Sugar Ray Robinson, cheered him lustily.

On June 10, 1946, while Johnson was driving up from the South to attend the Joe Louis–Billy Conn heavyweight title match, he lost control of his car and crashed into a utility pole. He died a few hours later at the age of 68. Despite the hard and often tragic circumstances of his life, he realized his ambition of making his mark in life—and made it possible for many other black fighters to realize their own dreams

The first black American to win an Olympic gold medal, James Cleveland Owens was born on September 12, 1913, in Oakville, Alabama. The youngest in a family of 10 children, James, nicknamed J.C., was a sickly child, prone to bouts of pneumonia and other ailments. His parents, Henry and Mary Emma, were former slaves who struggled to make a living by farming someone else's land. They could not afford decent medical care for young J.C., and they feared he would not survive long. Somehow he pulled through his many illnesses, and by the time he was six he was working the fields with his brothers and sisters and hiking the nine miles to Oakville's one-room schoolhouse.

When J.C. was 10 years old, the family moved north to Cleveland, Ohio, in search of a better life. The transition was difficult for the simple, religious folk from the rural South—but there was work for J.C.'s parents and older brothers, and soon the family enjoyed a level of comfort they had never dreamed of in Alabama. J.C. worked part-time in a cobbler's shop, and he also got to attend a real school. When he gave his name as J. C. Owens on his first day in class, the teacher misunderstood his Alabama drawl and wrote down "Jesse." He was too shy to correct her, and he remained Jesse Owens for the rest of his life.

By the time Jesse reached junior high school, he was a confirmed city boy, wise to the ways of the streets but unsure which direction he was going in. Then he met two people who changed his life. The first was Minnie Ruth Solomon, a young woman whose family had just come north from a farm in Alabama. Since he shared Ruth's background, Jesse was the ideal person to help her get used to Cleveland. Before long the two teenagers were in love, and though they were still too young to marry, the question was settled for both of them. The second important person who came into Jesse's life was Charles Riley, the track coach at Jesse's school. Jesse had not shown any special athletic promise at that point, but Riley saw some potential in him and invited him to try out for the track team.

After beefing up his diet (at Riley's expense) and going through a program to build up his body and his still-delicate lungs, Owens astonished the coach by running the 100-yard dash in 11 seconds, a remarkable time for a 15-year-old. Before long, Riley entered Owens in a variety of events, including the long jump and the high jump, and Owens excelled in them all.

If not for his mother, Owens would have had to leave school at this point, because the Great Depression of the 1930s had drastically reduced the family's income. But Mary Owens insisted that her son enroll at East Technical High School, where Charles Riley was soon hired as assistant track coach. Owens continued to progress under Riley's tutelage, often scoring more than half the team's points at track meets. Owens was named the captain of the team and was also elected student body president in the predominantly white school, a testament to his outgoing personality as well as his athletic brilliance.

In 1933, Owens entered Ohio State University, where he was given an unofficial scholarship, and came under the tutelage of track coach Larry Snyder. When Owens competed in his first Big Ten meet in early 1935, he immediately established his presence by winning three of the four events he entered. That May, at the Big Ten Championships, he astonished everyone by breaking five world records and tying another, a feat still unequaled in the annals of track and field.

Owens was propelled overnight into the role of a national sports star. Before he reaped the benefits of his new status, he took care of some unfinished business. Three years before, Ruth Solomon had given birth to a daughter. When her parents learned that Owens was the child's father, they refused to let Ruth see him again. The couple had been forced to live apart, although Owens sent money regularly for his daughter's support. Now that he had established himself, the Solomons relented; in July 1935, Jesse and Ruth Solomon were married in Cleveland.

The following year, Ohio State officials suspended Owens from the track team because of poor grades. He bore down and raised his average enough to be reinstated in time for the spring, when he ran 100 yards in a world-record time of 9.3 seconds. Dominating the sprints at the Olympic trials, Owens emerged as one of the mainstays of the American squad that journeyed to Berlin, Germany, for the 1936 Summer Olympics.

The Berlin Olympics were the most dramatic event of Owens's career, not only for the records he set but for the pride he brought to all Americans, especially blacks and other ethnic minorities. In 1936, Germany was ruled by Adolf Hitler and his Nazi party. The Nazis fostered the myth of a supposedly superior Aryan race, represented by blue-eyed, blond-haired men and women; they scorned and persecuted all other groups, including Jews and blacks. Hitler bragged that the 1936 Games would be a showcase of Aryan superiority.

Owens single-handedly shattered the Nazis' fantasies, winning his first gold medal with a time of 10.3 seconds in the 100-meter dash, thus tying the Olympic record he had set in a qualifying heat. Topping this feat, he went on to capture the long jump with a record-breaking leap of 26 feet 5 inches. Finally, Owens took his third medal with a record-shattering time of 20.7 in the 200-meter race. Despite the displeasure of their leaders, the German fans went wild over Owens, who became the star of the Games. In addition to his records, his close friendship with the German Luz Long, his biggest competitor in the long jump, exemplified the true Olympic ideals of sportsmanship and international understanding.

Owens returned home a celebrity, hailed in motorcades in New York, Cleveland, and Ohio's state capital, Columbus. He thought of returning to Ohio State, but the opportunity to cash in on his fame was too alluring to resist. His hopes of a movie contract did not pan out, but he was in demand for so many endorsements and banquets that he soon made a considerable sum of money, much of which he used to help his family. He realized, however, that a number of the things he was asked to do were beneath his dignity; perhaps the best-publicized among them was a race against a horse in Havana, Cuba. (With a 40-yard head start, Owens won.)

In the years that followed, Owens struggled continuously to turn his celebrity into a steady income for his family. In 1937, he went on tour as the leader of a 12-piece orchestra, then barnstormed with basketball and baseball teams, putting on running exhibitions when the opportunity presented itself. Unhappy about prolonged absences from his family, he soon found a job with the Cleveland recreation department and also opened a dry-cleaning business. Still, he struggled to make a living; then, in 1940, he suffered a double blow when his beloved mother died and the Internal Revenue Service got after him for back taxes, forcing him to close his business.

Regretting his failure to work harder as a student, Owens now determined to go back to Ohio State and earn his degree. Try as he would, it was too difficult for him to resume the role of a student, and he gave it up after a year. When the United States entered World War II in 1941, Owens was hired by the government to organize physical-fitness programs. Then he took an important and satisfying job with the Ford Motor Company in Detroit, looking after the social needs of the thousands of black workers on the Ford payroll.

Following the end of the war in 1945, Owens moved his family to Chicago and went into the public relations business, lending the luster of his still-famous name to a variety of companies. His business career was given an additional boost by the Associated Press in 1950, when they named him the greatest track-and-field athlete in history. Nevertheless, Owens was to watch with some sadness in the coming years as his records were broken by a new generation of athletes. His business success caused him to become rather conservative politically, and the black protest movement of the 1960s both surprised and annoyed him, causing him to say and write things that he later regretted.

Whatever his difficulties, Owens's spirits were never down for long. The one thing he could not overcome, however, was his health. His lungs, delicate in childhood, now succumbed to the ravages of a 30-year smoking habit. On March 31, 1980, Jesse Owens died of lung cancer in Tucson, Arizona. As an athlete and a man, he established standards that Americans still cherish, even after others have replaced him in the record books.

FRANK ROBINSON

Baseball's first black mana-
ger as well as one of its all-time great players, Frank
Robinson was born in Beaumont, Texas, on August
31, 1935. When he was very young his mother moved
the family to Oakland, California, where Frank grew
up in a racially mixed neighborhood. In 1947, when
Frank was 11 years old, Jackie Robinson became the

first African-American to play major league baseball. At the time, Frank had no thought of playing in the major leagues himself, but he was a good all-around athlete who played baseball, basketball, and football with an intensity that became his hallmark in later years.

When Frank was a 14-year-old junior high school student, he attracted the attention of George Powles, the baseball coach at a nearby school. Powles recruited Robinson for his American Legion team, which went on to win a national championship. While playing for Powles's team, Robinson was noticed by Bobby Mattick, a scout for the Chicago White Sox. When Mattick went to work for the Cincinnati Reds, he remembered Frank and offered him a contract with the Reds' Class C minor league team in Ogden, Utah. Upon graduating from McClymonds High School in 1953, Frank signed his first professional contract, receiving a $3,500 bonus and a salary of $400 a month.

Robinson had a fine season for the Ogden club, batting .348 and smacking 17 home runs. But the season was not a happy one. In addition to being away from home for the first time, he had his first real experience with racial prejudice. Ogden was virtually an all-white community, and members of other races were made to feel unwelcome. No one would rent Robinson a room in a private home, and he had to share a hotel room with teammate Chico Terry, a dark-skinned Latino who spoke little English. It was a depressing time for Robinson, but he made up his mind that he would put up with anything in order to reach the majors.

Robinson's play at Ogden earned him a promotion to the Columbia, South Carolina, Reds in the South Atlantic (Sally) League. In the South, where segregation was still in force, he was subjected to even further indignities. Again, he made up his mind to ignore the distractions and pushed himself to excel. He batted .336 that year and looked so impressive during spring training in 1955 that the Reds named him their starting left fielder. However, Robinson had injured his shoulder playing winter ball and soon found that his ability to throw and swing the bat was severely hampered. He was sent back to Columbia, where he continued to struggle.

Finally, frustrated by his sore shoulder and by the racial taunts of the fans, Robinson was ready to quit baseball. Fortunately, Marv Williams, the only other black player on the team, convinced him to stick with it. Before long his shoulder improved; he tore up the Sally League for the rest of the season, and 1956 found him in left field for the Cincinnati club.

Robinson fulfilled all the Reds' expectations by batting .290, hitting 38 homers, and driving in 83 runs—named to the All-Star team in July, he was a unanimous choice for the National League Rookie of the Year Award. He quickly gained a reputation as a fierce competitor who would slide into bases with his spikes flashing and go out of his way to take out infielders. Opposing players often disliked him, but they also respected him, because he could take punishment as well as dish it out. During his first year, for example, Robinson was hit by pitches 20 times—his only response was to bear down harder and crowd the plate even more.

Each year, Robinson improved as a ballplayer, and by 1959 he was the highest-paid player on the Cincinnati squad. In 1961, he led the team to the National League pennant and was named the league's Most Valuable Player. But away from the playing field, he was treated like a second-class citizen: when he and his wife, Barbara, decided to buy a house, they found that because of the color of their skin they were unwelcome in any of Cincinnati's more affluent neighborhoods.

Though all the Reds players acknowledged Robinson as their leader, his relations with the team's management were often difficult. Each year, Robinson battled for the kind of contract he thought he deserved, and the Reds officials apparently grew tired of his combativeness. After the 1965 season, they traded him to the Baltimore Orioles of the American League.

In some of their public comments, the Reds implied that Robinson was over the hill at the age of 30. He quickly proved them wrong by batting .316, blasting 49 homers, and driving in 122 runs, leading the league in all three categories. More important, his fiery determination drove the Orioles all the way to the world championship. Robinson was named Most Valuable Player for both the regular season and the World Series, becoming the first (and still the only) player in baseball history to win the MVP Award in both leagues.

Robinson had one more ambition to fulfill—he wanted to become baseball's first black manager. He took his first step in 1968, when he was selected to manage the Santurce club in the Puerto Rican winter league. It was not the majors, but it gave Robinson the chance to show that he knew how to run a ball club. He also dispelled the myth, often advanced by opponents of change in baseball, that white players would refuse to take orders from a black manager.

Of course, Robinson was not quite ready to hang up his spikes. He led the Orioles to another world championship in 1970, hit his 500th home run in 1971, and then moved on to the Los Angeles Dodgers and the California Angels as his career began to wind down. Each winter he went back to manage in Puerto Rico, and by this time he was growing impatient when he was passed over for vacant managerial jobs. Finally, while Robinson was playing for the Cleveland Indians in 1975, the break came: the team dismissed its manager and placed Robinson at the helm.

Now that he had realized his ambition, Robinson found managing an often frustrating experience. As a superstar with the Reds and Orioles, he had played the game so hard that the other players had to follow his example. As a manager, however, he had to find other ways of motivating his team. He was puzzled and annoyed when he discovered that few of his players shared his all-out approach to the game. The Indians finished in fourth place in both 1975 and 1976, and when the team got off to a poor start in 1977, Robinson was fired.

Critics of baseball's hiring practices felt that Robinson had not been given a fair chance, and he agreed—but he refused to hang his head. Instead, Robinson managed in Mexico during the winter and went back to the Orioles as a coach. Meanwhile, two other well-qualified African-Americans were offered managerial jobs: Larry Doby with the White Sox and Maury Wills with the Seattle Mariners.

In 1981, the San Francisco Giants offered Robinson another chance to manage, and he repaid their confidence by guiding the team to a first-place finish the following year. For his efforts he was voted National League Manager of the Year. Also in 1982, he was inducted into the Baseball Hall of Fame along with baseball's all-time home-run king, Hank Aaron. After this peak, however, it was all downhill for the Giants. When the team finished last in 1984, Robinson found himself out of a job once again. He returned to the Orioles, first as a coach and then as a front-office official.

With the Orioles spinning their wheels early in the 1988 season, the team asked Robinson to take charge in the dugout. Making use of the experience he had gained in his previous jobs, he had the young team contending for the pennant the following season. Once again, he was named Manager of the Year. But the old maxim that managers are hired to be fired caught up with Robinson again in May 1991, when the Baltimore ownership attempted to charge up a slumping team by changing managers.

Robinson went back into the Baltimore front office—as an assistant general manager—without having fulfilled his ambition to be the first black manager to win a World Series. He will never realize that particular dream because Cito Gaston of the Toronto Blue Jays got there first in 1992. But Gaston's triumph also belonged to Robinson, because once again the former slugger, with his drive and determination, had showed others how to reach the heights.

JACKIE ROBINSON

The first black American to play major league baseball, Jack Roosevelt Robinson was born on January 31, 1919. The grandson of a slave, Jackie was the youngest of five children born to Mallie and Jerry Robinson, who lived a sharecropper's existence in Cairo, Georgia. When Jackie was six months old, his father abandoned the family, and Mallie Robinson moved with her children to Pasadena, California.

While their mother worked as a cleaning woman to support the family, the Robinson children went to school and played sports in their free time. One of the brothers, Mack, became a world-class sprinter and eventually competed in the 1936 Olympics in Berlin, Germany, finishing second to Jesse Owens, who won the gold medal.

As a youth, Jackie associated with a gang of local boys who committed minor offenses. With the intervention of concerned members of his community, Jackie left the gang and volunteered to teach Sunday school at his church. Jackie excelled in athletics at John Muir Technical High School, earning letters in football, basketball, baseball, and track.

His athletic prowess earned him a scholarship to the University of California at Los Angeles, which he entered in 1939. Though Jackie felt out of place at such a wealthy school, he certainly fit in on the playing field, and he became UCLA's first four-letter man. He was the top scorer in the basketball conference two years in a row, won the national championship in the long jump, and was named an all-American halfback in football.

Despite his success in athletics, Jackie left UCLA in the spring of 1941 because he believed an education would not help a black man get a job and he wanted to help relieve some of the financial burden his mother was carrying. He became an athletic director for the National Youth Administration, where he greatly enjoyed working with disadvantaged children.

His career was cut short when he was drafted by the U.S. Army in 1942 and sent to Fort Riley, Kansas, for basic training. Although Robinson was qualified to attend officer candidate school (OCS), he and other capable soldiers were passed over because they were black. Disappointed and disgusted, Robinson complained to Joe Louis, the heavyweight boxing champion, who was also at Fort Riley. Louis used his influence to get Robinson and the other black soldiers admitted to OCS, and in January 1943, Robinson became a second lieutenant.

His new stripes meant little difference in the amount of discrimination Robinson encountered in the army. His problems increased when he was transferred to Fort Hood, Texas, in 1944. He was almost court-martialed for his refusal to sit in the back of a bus he had been riding on, but he was found to be acting within his rights. However, the army labeled him a troublemaker and would not permit him to fight overseas, and he was granted an honorable discharge.

Robinson returned home more defiant than ever and joined the Kansas City Monarchs, a Negro League baseball team. Playing in the Negro Leagues was difficult; living conditions were terrible, players were discriminated against in hotels and restaurants, and talented ballplayers never received the recognition they deserved.

Branch Rickey, the president of the Brooklyn Dodgers, saved Robinson from this obscurity when he persuaded him to leave the Monarchs for the Montreal Royals, the Dodgers' minor league team. One of baseball's most innovative executives, Rickey had decided it was time to break baseball's color barrier, and he was looking for a special player to do the job. The first black man in major league baseball had to be an individual able to deal with the discrimination and abuse he would most certainly encounter, and he must be disciplined enough not to let anything affect his game.

After seeing him play with the Monarchs during the summer of 1945, Rickey decided that Jackie Robinson was the man he was looking for and offered the ballplayer a starting salary of $600 a month and a signing bonus of $3,500. Robinson received a bonus in his personal life when he married Rachel Isum— whom he had first met in 1940 while they were both students at UCLA—in the winter of 1946.

In April 1946, Robinson made his minor league debut with the Montreal Royals against the Jersey City Giants. The stands were packed with fans who saw Robinson hit a three-run home run and steal two bases, helping the Royals to victory over the Giants. Robinson continued his high level of play and became a popular sports figure in the Royals' hometown.

Outside Canada, people reacted quite differently to the rising young star. Racial slurs were thrown at him during games by fans and players alike, and he was pulled from games due to laws prohibiting interracial athletics. These incidents began to take their toll on the young player, and the pressure caused him to fall into a hitting slump. The Montreal fans, however, came to the ballpark to root for Robinson, and their support helped him shake out of his slump and lead his team to the league championship.

Rickey decided it was time to move Robinson to the major leagues, and on April 15, 1947, Jackie stepped up to the plate as a major league player for the first time. At first his performance was mediocre, and fans as well as Robinson's fellow players doubted whether he was ready for the big time.

During a game with the Philadelphia Phillies, Robinson was shocked by a constant stream of racial epithets from the Phillies' dugout. Robinson's calm and poise in the face of this onslaught won him the respect of his teammates as well as the New York sportswriters, who condemned the Phillies' players for their behavior.

Support from his teammates and the fans helped Robinson improve his performance on the field. Black fans in particular flocked to the ballpark to see Robinson play. Robinson helped his team win the National League championship that year, and although the Dodgers lost the World Series to their rivals, the New York Yankees, Robinson was honored with the title of Rookie of the Year.

Robinson's variety of skills soon made him one of the best players in the game. A fine hitter under any

circumstances who batted over .300 lifetime, he became even more difficult to retire in clutch situations.
In 1949, he led the league in batting. In the field,
Robinson possessed the versatility and intelligence to
play several different positions superbly; though
primarily a second baseman, he played often at third
base, first base, and the outfield as well.

But Robinson was at his absolute best on the base
paths. Powerfully built, at nearly six feet tall and
almost 200 pounds, he was one of the game's swiftest
runners, and the sight of him dancing recklessly off
base in his peculiar pigeon-toed gate, defying the
opposition to hold him close, soon became one of the
game's most thrilling sights. He twice led the league
in stolen bases, exhibiting an exceedingly rare ability
to swipe home as well as an aptitude for escaping
rundowns.

Taken as a whole, Robinson's skills helped make the
Dodgers a perennial National League powerhouse,
and in 1949 he was voted the league's Most Valuable
Player. As he settled into consistent excellence on the
field, his home life also became more settled when he
and his wife, Rachel, moved to a suburb in St. Albans,
New York, with their son, Jackie, Jr., and their
daughter, Sharon.

Robinson's happiness was marred by the retirement
of Branch Rickey as president of the Dodgers. The
new president, Walter O'Malley, resented Robinson
for Jackie's continued loyalty to Rickey. The two had
a strained relationship throughout Robinson's years
on the team.

After his rookie year, Robinson became one of the most outspoken athletes of the time. While he was normally respectful and soft-spoken, he refused to remain silent when he thought he was being treated unfairly. Supported by Ford Frick, the baseball commissioner, Robinson felt free to speak out on any racial issues he felt needed to be addressed.

In 1955, the Dodgers finally beat the New York Yankees in the World Series, earning their only world championship. The following year was Robinson's last as a major league player and the last for the Dodgers in Brooklyn, as O'Malley decided to move the team west, to Los Angeles.

After his retirement, Robinson became the vice-president of community relations for the Chock Full O'Nuts coffee company. He enjoyed his work in building up the company's name and reputation within the community. He became more active in politics, business, and the civil rights movement and became a spokesman for the NAACP. In January 1962, he was inducted into the Baseball Hall of Fame.

Jackie Robinson died of a heart attack on October 24, 1972. His outstanding athletic ability, inner strength, and immense personal dignity had allowed him to triumph over racial prejudice; he remains a model to all those who fight to see their dreams and the dreams of others become reality.

BILL RUSSELL

The first black American to become coach of a National Basketball Association (NBA) team was born William Felton Russell on February 12, 1934, in Monroe, Louisiana.

Young Bill Russell was a member of a tightly knit family. His father, known as Mister Charlie, worked for a paper bag company and was respected within Monroe's black community for his willingness to stand firm for his beliefs. Mrs. Russell, the former Katie King, was as strong willed as her husband and very affectionate with Bill and his older brother, Charlie. Both parents stressed the importance of education and encouraged their two sons to concentrate on their schoolwork.

Life in the Deep South was not easy for blacks, especially strong-willed people like the Russells. After a gas-station attendant pointed a rifle at him for not being more respectful to whites, Mister Charlie decided to move his family to Oakland, California, where he and his wife took jobs in a shipyard. The family moved into an ostensibly integrated housing project—blacks lived in one section, whites in another—where Bill first learned to play basketball.

After his mother died from influenza in the fall of 1946, young Bill grew subdued and introverted, and he spent much of his time reading. His withdrawal grew more profound with his failure to make any sports teams at Hoover Junior High School. But at the age of 16, the boy experienced a surge of confidence, and he decided to try out for the junior varsity basketball team at McClymonds High School, where Charlie had been a star athlete.

Although Bill was awkward and largely unskilled, the team's coach, George Powles, worked with him and encouraged him to practice to improve his game. Though Bill excelled in drills that required only running and jumping, he had problems with ball handling. Still, as the result of much practice, by his junior year he had earned a spot on the varsity team.

Russell's game improved during his senior year, and even though he was still only a mediocre player, he was part of a winning basketball team. After graduating in January 1952, he was chosen for a team of high school all-stars that toured the Pacific Northwest. Now six feet five inches tall and 160 pounds, Russell learned much from watching his teammates. He mastered the art of rebounding and taught himself to excel on defense.

Upon his return to Oakland after the all-star tour, Russell became an apprentice sheet-metal worker at the San Francisco Naval Yard. In his spare time, he played in pickup basketball games in local schoolyards, and his game improved dramatically. Soon a scout who had seen him play arranged for him to receive a scholarship to the University of San Francisco (USF).

At USF, Russell took full advantage of the many opportunities open to him. His primary emphasis was his education, but he also found time to work on his game, receiving special help in that regard from his coach, Phil Woolpert, and his roommate and teammate K. C. Jones.

In a very short time, Russell became a very fine player indeed, the best "big man" in the country and the primary reason why USF was able to win national championships in 1955 and 1956. Though an adept player at the collegiate level who scored over 20 points a game, Russell was at best a merely adequate shooter who truly dominated games through rebounding and defense, especially the blocked shot, which as a component of his game was as much psychological tactic as physical feat. Russell might only block a few shots in any game, but his uncanny timing made opponents always aware of his presence on the court. Before him, the game's big men had generally been plodding, mechanical, earthbound players. Russell, by contrast, was frighteningly quick and a great jumper, an unprecedented combination of size and athleticism.

Russell also possessed a superb understanding of the dynamics of team basketball, an insight that would make him the winningest player ever to lace up a pair of sneakers. He followed his two national championships at USF with a stint as a member (with K. C. Jones) of the U.S. Olympic team that copped the gold medal at Melbourne, Australia, in autumn 1956. His winning streak continued after his return to the United States when, on December 9, 1956, he married Rose Swisher and then joined the Boston Celtics of the NBA. The rookie then carried the Celtics to their first championship.

Though Russell and the Celtics relinquished their crown the following year, when a sprained ankle kept him on the sidelines for the finals, with the 1958–59 season he and his teammates (who included his old friend K. C. Jones) began an unprecedented (and still unmatched) streak of eight consecutive NBA championships. That run came to an end in 1967, but the Celtics returned to the top in 1968 and remained there until Russell retired as a player following the 1968–69 season. In his 13 years in the NBA, Russell and the Celtics won the championship 11 times, a record of success unmatched by any individual or team. During those 13 years, Russell's surrounding cast changed several times, leaving him as the one constant in the Celtics' success. He was voted the NBA's Most Valuable Player (MVP) five times.

Off the court, Russell was an equally influential athlete. His public campaign against racism began with a personal slight: despite winning the league's MVP Award for the 1957–58 season, Russell was left off the NBA's all-league team as a result, he believed, of racial prejudice on the part of the selectors. (Though the NBA had been integrated in 1950—the Celtics had been the first team to sign a black player—the league was still, in the late 1950s, a predominantly white institution.)

Russell soon turned his attention to off-court racism. An outspoken advocate of the civil rights movement at a time when few prominent athletes were willing to take positions on social issues, Russell took part in the March on Washington in 1963 and participated in numerous civil rights demonstrations in the South. He also challenged the self-satisfaction of white fans who cheered his every move in the Boston Garden when he publicly proclaimed Boston to be the most racist city in America and delineated the examples of the prejudice he and his family had endured despite his somewhat privileged social status.

Despite his uncompromising positions, Russell was rewarded for 10 years of exceptional service to the Celtics in 1966, when he was asked to succeed the legendary Boston mastermind, Arnold "Red" Auerbach, as coach of the team. The appointment was testimony to Russell's fierce pride, unyielding will to win, and comprehensive knowledge of the game; even so, he realized that as the first black head coach in the history of the NBA, he would be regarded as having much to prove.

As a coach, Russell was most fortunate in one key regard: he could still call on his own services as a player. Still, his dual responsibilities—as a player, he had to concentrate on his own game, and as coach, he also had to concentrate on the job his teammates were doing—required some adjustment on the part of himself and his teammates. Despite 60 regular-season victories, in his first year at the helm the Celtics' long string of championships came to an end at the hands of the Philadelphia 76ers, led by Wilt Chamberlain, Russell's great rival over much of his career.

Russell and the Celtics were vindicated the following year when they beat the 76ers and reclaimed the NBA title. Off the court, Russell continued his fight against racial prejudice, but his many hours away from his family took a toll on his family life, and he and his wife separated in 1969. That year, the aging Celtics, despite a poor fourth-place finish in the regular season, regrouped in the playoffs, allowing Russell to claim his final championship. Worn out, he retired as both player and coach and moved to Los Angeles, where he landed several cameo roles on various television shows. He also did a number of very well received lecture tours of the United States.

He made his return to the game in the early 1970s as an analyst on national-television basketball broadcasts, a capacity in which he eventually served for three networks. During this time, he also began to be awarded various honors for his playing career.

Though the recognition made him uncomfortable—he had played for the pleasure of the game, he said, not for personal rewards—the honors continued nonetheless. In spite of his protests, his uniform was retired by the Boston Celtics in March 1972, and he was inducted into the Basketball Hall of Fame in 1974.

Despite initial hesitation, in 1973, Russell returned to the NBA as coach and general manager of the Seattle SuperSonics. Though Seattle initially experienced some success under his tutelage, Russell found it difficult to relate to the new generation of professional basketball players, and he left the franchise in 1977 to resume his broadcasting and lecturing careers. His second autobiography, *Second Wind*, was published in 1979, 13 years after his first autobiography, *Go Up for Glory*.

Though a coaching and executive stint with the Sacramento Kings in the late 1980s proved disastrously unsuccessful, Bill Russell's winning legacy remains the standard by which every new, would-be basketball champion is still measured.

❧ FURTHER READING ❧

Arthur Ashe

Ashe, Arthur. *A Hard Road to Glory: A History of the African-American Athlete.* 3 vols. New York: Warner Books, 1988.

Ashe, Arthur, with Neil Amdur. *Off the Court.* New York: New American Library, 1981.

Weissberg, Ted. *Arthur Ashe.* New York: Chelsea House, 1991.

Chuck Cooper

George, Nelson. *Elevating the Game: The History and Aesthetics of Black Men in Basketball.* New York: Simon & Schuster, 1992.

Althea Gibson

Biracree, Tom. *Althea Gibson.* New York: Chelsea House, 1989.

Gibson, Althea. *I Always Wanted To Be Somebody.* New York: Harper & Brothers, 1958.

———. *So Much To Live For.* New York: Putnam, 1968.

Jack Johnson

Jakoubek, Robert. *Jack Johnson.* New York: Chelsea House, 1990.

Johnson, Jack. *Jack Johnson Is a Dandy.* New York: Chelsea House, 1969.

Roberts, Randy. *Papa Jack: Jack Johnson and the Era of White Hopes.* New York: Free Press, 1983.

Jesse Owens

Gentry, Tony. *Jesse Owens.* New York: Chelsea House, 1990.

Owens, Jesse. *I Have Changed.* New York: Morrow, 1972.

———. *Jesse: A Spiritual Autobiography.* Plainfield, NJ: Logos International, 1978.

Frank Robinson

Macht, Norman L. *Frank Robinson.* New York: Chelsea House, 1991.

Robinson, Frank, and Berry Stainback. *Extra Innings.* New York: McGraw-Hill, 1988.

Robinson, Frank, and Dave Anderson. *Frank: The First Year.* New York: Holt, Rinehart & Winston, 1976.

Jackie Robinson

Frommer, Harvey. *Jackie Robinson.* New York: Franklin Watts, 1984.

Robinson, Jackie. *I Never Had It Made.* New York: Putnam, 1972.

Scott, Richard. *Jackie Robinson.* New York: Chelsea House, 1987.

Bill Russell

Russell, Bill, and Taylor Branch. *Second Wind: Memoirs of an Opinionated Man.* New York: Random House, 1979.

❧ INDEX ☙

❧ PICTURE CREDITS ❧

RICHARD RENNERT has edited the nearly 100 volumes in Chelsea House's award-winning BLACK AMERICANS OF ACHIEVEMENT series, which tells the stories of black men and women who have helped shape the course of modern history. He is also the author of several sports biographies, including *Henry Aaron*, *Jesse Owens*, and *Jackie Robinson*. He is a graduate of Haverford College in Haverford, Pennsylvania.